Text copyright © 1997 by Ray Bradbury
Illustrations copyright © 1997 by Louise Reinoehl Max

This is a Peregrine Smith Book, published by
Gibbs Smith, Publisher
P.O. Box 667
Layton, Utah 84041

Design by David Charlsen, San Francisco, CA
Printed and bound in China

Library of Congress Cataloging-in-Publication Data
Bradbury, Ray, 1920–
    Dogs think that every day is Christmas / by Ray Bradbury ; illustrated by Louise Reinoehl Max.
      p.   cm.
   ISBN 0-87905-753-X
   1. Dogs—poetry. I. Title.
PS3503.R167D64 1997
811'.54—dc21   97-10115
                                                CIP

First edition
00 99 98 97   5 4 3 2 1

A few months before the holidays in 1995, I heard someone say, "Dogs think that every day is Christmas." Struck by what seemed an obvious truth, I went up to the next half dozen dogs I met and said, "What day is this?" Their response, "If you gotta ask, you'll never know!"

I beat a hasty retreat and wrote this poem, showed it to the dogs, and they all said, "That's more *like* it!"

I have never since asked any good canine friend the time of day when all the while I knew it was Christ's birthday.

Dogs, it is obvious, have played a great part in my life. I have had all sorts, from half-breed dachshunds low down to the ground, to fluff-balls that grew giant size above the earth. Each I have loved intemperately, madly. While admiring the originality of a friend who called his male and female pals Dog and Dogma, mine loped around with little more than Pete or Ralph or Sam. My grandma's dog Teddy followed me through life from the time I was born until I was ten. When he died in 1930, some small part of my soul flopped over and went into the backyard burial ground with him. His bones joined the bones of other pooches named Bozo and Hash.

When my family headed west in 1934 (my dad was searching for work in the Great Depression) the worst thing was leaving my dog Pete behind. Even worse was the terrible thing I had done to Pete in an earlier year. Just before Christmas, Pete vanished, ran off somewhere in the winter snows and left me, destroyed, to weep. He was gone for three or four nights, until one night, just after midnight, I heard a scratching/whining at the door. Flinging it wide, I found Pete scrambling for affection, yipping, frosted with sleet, a miserable refugee from the falling snow. I dragged him in and fell to my knees, embracing him and weeping all over again.

And then, my God, I did a terrible thing.

I struck him.

I hit him not once or twice but three or four times, and as my fists went home I cried, "Why did you leave me? Why did you run away? How could you *do* that?!" and kept shouting that and striking him, until suddenly I collapsed and grabbed hold and wept even more, sobbing, "Oh, Pete, I didn't mean that. I'm sorry. Forgive me. It was just that I thought you would never come back, Pete. I thought you were dead. Forgive! Forgive!"

And Pete, of course, whining, let me hold tight, and he forgave.

But it haunted me for the rest of my life that I could have done that to him, that sweet, good-natured friend, my pal forever. It bothered me so much, in fact, that fifty years later I had to write a story called "Bless Me, Father, For I Have Sinned," all about a priest who, one Christmas Eve, hears the confession of a vagrant parishioner who asks to be pardoned for striking his dog when he was a boy.

"Will God forgive me, do *you* forgive me, Father?" the stranger asks from the other side of the confessional.

"*I* do, *God* does," says the priest. "For the same thing happened to me when I was a child. I struck my lost dog when he came home on Christmas Eve. Now, let us forgive one another. The bells have just struck midnight, Christ is born. Come into the vestry and have a glass of wine."

But when the priest steps out of the confessional and opens the opposite door, there is no one there. He looks up at a mirror across the hall, sees himself there, and gestures to his image—a sign of forgiveness. At last, he has laid the ghost of his animal friend to rest.

Except that there is no rest.

I told this story at a library lecture one evening a few years ago, and toward the end, tears were rolling down my cheeks. I was twelve years old again and Pete was alive and I had struck him. I had to stop, in front of that audience, and get back my breath before I could continue.

Even as I write this, the old tears come back. I wonder how many times I must tell this story before my regrets will cease.

Enough, I think you see from all this the part that these loves of my life have played and continue to play.

In Santa Cruz a few years back, I stayed overnight at the home of a ladyfriend who owned and operated a peacock, a goat, a horse, six cats, and a dozen dogs. Sleeping over that night, the dogs swarmed on my bed—clean, intelligent, and well-behaved. I slept, all happiness, under a blanket of dogs. Top *that!*

To paraphrase the opening paragraph of Melville's *Moby Dick* — when it is a cold, grey, melancholy night in my soul, I do not go to sea. Never that, no. I stand me up, turn me around, and head off for . . .

The nearest Dog Show, where, surrounded by a dozen score of fabulous beasts, my soul is warmed, my heart knows peace, and I come forth all smiles and laughter.

—**Ray Bradbury**
March 7, 1997

Dogs think that every day
is Christmas;

They lap it with their
necktie tongues,

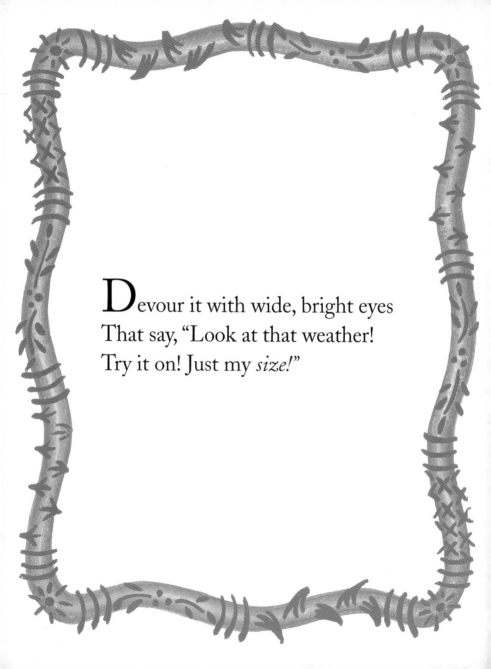

Devour it with wide, bright eyes
That say, "Look at that weather!
Try it on! Just my *size!*"

They lean out car windows
Like drunks at bars, snuffing gin,
While drivers in the same cars,
   running, lose,
They *win!*

They mark each tree in passing
Just to let the world know
"I was here. Do you *see?* I was here!"

From the start of a glorious season

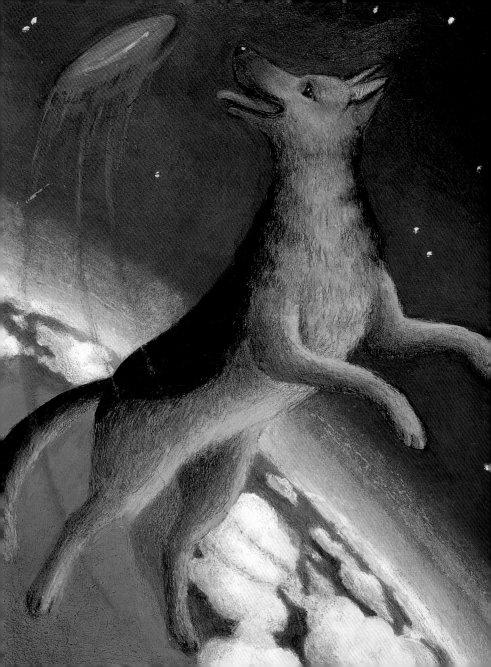

To the end of a marvelous year.

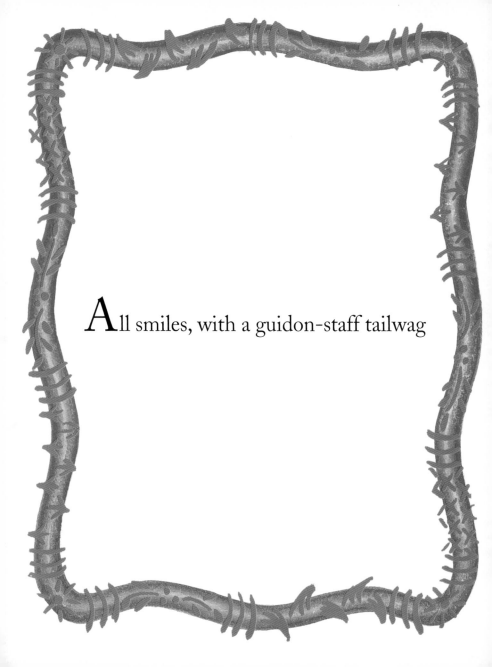

All smiles, with a guidon-staff tailwag

They silently shout, "Gee whiz!"

Because dogs wake each day
to Christmas.

And, matter of fact,
I'll be damned,

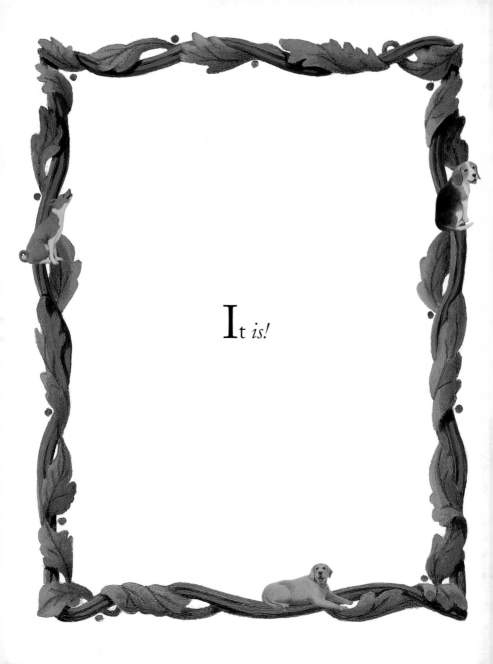

It $is!$

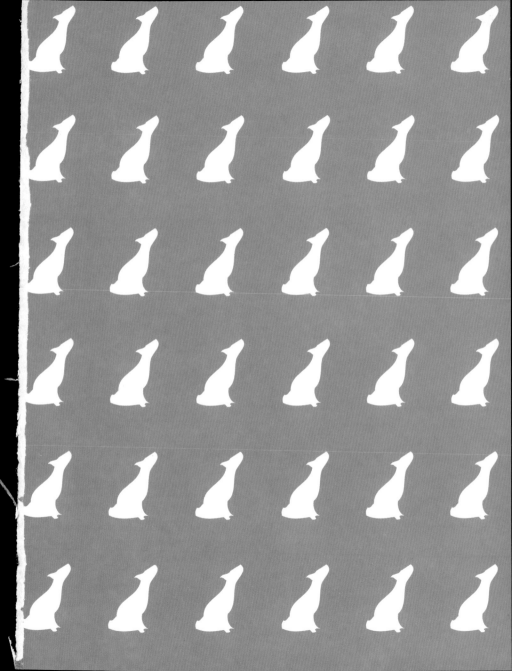

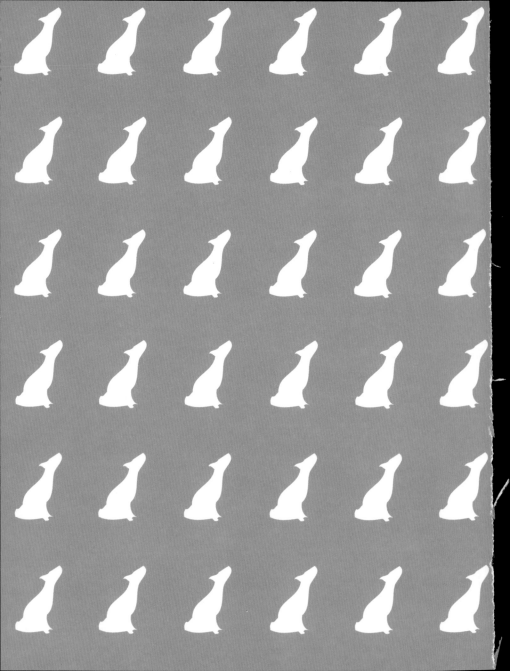